SMOKING MEAT ELECTRIC SMOKER COOKBOOK

ULTIMATE SMOKER COOKBOOK FOR REAL PITMASTERS, IRRESISTIBLE RECIPES FOR YOUR ELECTRIC SMOKER

BOOK 2

BY ADAM JONES

TABLE OF CONTENTS

INTRODUCTION

Electric smokers very easily provide the option to smoke meats through an easy-to-use and accessible interface. Where there is a smoke, there is a flavor. Smoking meat or making BBQ is not only a means of cooking but for some individuals and classy enthusiasts, this is a form of Art! Or dare I say a form of lifestyle!Enthusiasts all around the world have been experimenting and dissecting the secrets of perfectly smoked meat for decades now, and in our golden age, perhaps they have cracked it up completely!In our age, the technique of Barbequing or Smoking meat has been perfected to such a level, that a BBQ Grill is pretty much an essential amenity found in all backyard or sea-beach parties!

This is the drinking fountain for the more hip and adventurous people, who prefer to have a nice chat with their friends and families while smoking up a few batches of Burger Patty for them to enjoy. But here's the thing, while this art might seem like a very easy form of cooking which only requires you to flip meats over and over! Mastering it might be a little bit difficult if you don't know have the proper information with you. This guide is an essential book for beginners who want to smoke meat without needing expert help from others. This book offers detailed guidance obtained by years of smoking meat, includes clear instructions and step-by-step directions for every recipe. This is the only guide you will ever need to professionally smoke a variety of food. The book includes photographs of every finished meal to make your job easier. Whether you are a beginner meat smoker or looking to go beyond the basics, the book gives you the tools and tips you need to start that perfectly smoked meat. Smoking is something has withstood the test of time, it will continue to stand the test of time for years to come. Not only is it a method to preserve your catch or kill, but it's also one of if not the best-tasting food there is.

CHAPTER 1: POULTRY RECIPES
SMOKED CHICKEN TENDERS

Craving for chicken nuggets? This is the closest you are going to get with your amazing electric smoker! Just give it a try, you just might be delightfully surprised with the result!

SERVING: 8

PREP TIME: 10 MINUTES

SMOKE TIME: 60 MINUTES

PREFERRED WOOD: HICKORY

INGREDIENTS

- 4 pound of chicken tenders
- ½ a cup of soy sauce
- ½ a cup of vegetable oil
- ¼ cup of water
- 1 and a ½ tablespoon of sesame seeds
- 2 teaspoon of minced garlic
- ¾ teaspoon of freshly grated peeled ginger root

- ¼ teaspoon of Cajun seasoning
- Salt as needed

COOKING DIRECTIONS

1. Take a medium-sized bowl and add soy sauce, water, vegetable oil, sesame seeds, oil, garlic, Cajun seasoning, ginger and ½ a teaspoon of salt

2. Mix them well

3. Add the tenders in a re-sealable bag alongside the marinade and allow it to marinade overnight for about ours, make sure to give the bag a turn at least two times to ensure that it is properly marinated

4. Prepare your smokers water pan accordingly and pre-heated the smoker to 225 degrees Fahrenheit/107 degree Celsius

5. Take a medium-sized bowl and fill it up with your 3-4 handful of the woods and allow them to soak

6. Remove the tenders from the marinade and place them on the middle rack of your smoker

7. Smoke and cook for 60 minutes more until the internal temperature reaches 165 degrees Fahrenheit/73 degree Celsius making sure to replace the woods after every 15 minutes

8. Sprinkle some salt and enjoy!

EXTREME RED WINGS

If the previous red wings failed to the job for you, then this one is sure to turn you into a fire-breathing dragon!

SERVING: **8**

PREP TIME: **10** MINUTES

SMOKE TIME: **90** MINUTES

PREFERRED WOOD: HICKORY

INGREDIENTS

- 5 pound of chicken wings
- Salt as needed
- Pepper as needed
- Cajun seasoning
- 1 cup of hot sauce
- 1 cup of ketchup
- 1 stick of butter
- 1 teaspoon of garlic powder

COOKING DIRECTIONS

1. Season the chicken with salt, Cajun seasoning, and pepper

2. Prepare your smokers water pan accordingly and pre-heated the smoker to 250 degrees Fahrenheit/121 degree Celsius

3. Smoke and cook for 60 minutes more until the internal temperature reaches 165 degrees Fahrenheit/73 degree Celsius making sure to replace the woods after every 15 minutes

4. Take a saucepan and place it over medium heat

5. Add butter and melt it

6. Whisk in hot sauce, ketchup, garlic powder and simmer on LOW for 15-20 minutes

7. Remove the wings from the smoker and transfer them to an aluminum pan

8. Pour the sauce over the chicken

9. Return them to your smoker and smoke for another 30 minutes

10. Remove the wings and serve hot!

COOL SMOKED BUTTER CHICKEN

Succulent designed chicken pieces dripping with butter, what more do you need?

SERVING: 8

PREP TIME: 30 MINUTES

SMOKE TIME: 180 MINUTES

PREFERRED WOOD: PECAN

INGREDIENTS

- 2 pound of boneless and skinless chicken breast cut up into 1 inch pieces
- 5 tablespoon of divided butter
- 1 cup of sour cream
- 1 tablespoon of fresh squeezed lemon juice
- 2 tablespoon of divide chili powder
- 2 and a ½ tablespoon of Garam masala

13

- 2 tablespoon + 2 tablespoon f minced garlic cloves
- 1 tablespoon of + 2 tablespoon of freshly grated ginger
- 1 medium sized minced onion
- 1 seeded and minced jalapeno chile
- 1 tablespoon of sugar
- 1 teaspoon of ground coriander
- 28 ounce can of crushed tomatoes
- 1 tablespoon of tomato paste
- ¾ cup of heavy cream
- Cooked rice for serving
- Naan bread for serving

COOKING DIRECTIONS

1. Take a 1 gallon zip bag and add the chicken breast

2. Add 3 tablespoon of melt butter alongside sour cream, lemon juice, 1 tablespoon of chili powder, 1 tablespoon of Garam masala, 2 teaspoon of garlic, 2 teaspoon of ginger, 1 teaspoon of salt

3. Seal up the bag and massage the bag gently to ensure that the chicken is coated well

4. Allow it to chill for 1 -3 hours

5. Prepare your smokers water pan accordingly and pre-heated the smoker to 250 degree Fahrenheit/121 degree Celsius

6. Take a medium-sized bowl and fill it up with your 3-4 handful of the woods and allow them to soak

7. Pour the chicken and marinade into a 10 inch cast iron skillet and place it over the smoker

8. Cook for 30 minutes, making sure to stir after 15 minutes

9. While the chicken is being cooked, take another medium skillet and add 2 tablespoon of butter, 2 tablespoon of garlic, onion and jalapeno

10. Cook over medium-high heat for 3-5 minutes until the onions are translucent

11. Stir in sugar, coriander and 1 tablespoon of chili powder,1 and a ½ tablespoon of Garam masala,1 tablespoon of ginger, 1 teaspoon of salt

12. Cook for 1 minute to allow the flavors to be released

13. Stir in crushed tomatoes, heavy cream and tomato paste

14. Bring the whole mixture to a boil

15. Lower down the heat to low and simmer for 5 minutes, making sure to keep stirring it occasionally

16. Remove the heavy and the cast iron skillet from the smoker

17. Pour sauce into the cast-iron skillet with chicken and stir well

18. Return the chicken skillet back to the smoker

19. Close the smoker door and add some more chips to the loading bay

20. Stir and cook for 30 minutes more until the internal temperature reaches 165 degree Fahrenheit/73 degree Celsius and then cook for another 1 hour

21. Remove and serve the meal with rice and Naan.

CHICKEN CAESAR WRAPS

Visit the ancient times of Greeks and gobble up a wonderful chicken meal wrapped up like a Shawarma. If a party snack is what you desire, this is what you need!

SERVING: 8

PREP TIME: 10 MINUTES

SMOKE TIME: 60 MINUTES

PREFERRED WOOD: HICKORY

INGREDIENTS

- 2 pieces of chicken breasts
- Romaine Hearts
- 1 diced tomato
- Parmesan cheese as needed
- Caesar dressing
- Salt as needed
- Garlic powder as needed
- 4 large pieces of tortillas

COOKING DIRECTIONS

1. Prepare your smokers water pan accordingly and pre-heated the smoker to 225 degrees Fahrenheit/107 degree Celsius

2. Take a medium-sized bowl and fill it up with your 3-4 handful of the woods and allow them to soak

3. Season the chicken breast with pepper, garlic powder, and salt

4. Smoke and cook for 60 minutes more until the internal temperature reaches 165 degrees Fahrenheit/73 degree Celsius making sure to replace the woods after every 15 minutes

5. Heat up the tortillas on your stove in a pan

6. Remove the tortillas from the pan and lay them on a flat surface

7. Layer the salad, sliced up smoked chicken and tomatoes on top

8. Roll up and have fun!

LEMONY PEPPER CHICKENS

A smoked chicken meal that blends seamlessly blends the flavors of pepper and lemon and packs them up in a beautiful mixture. Yum yum!

SERVING: 8

PREP TIME: 10 MINUTES

MARINATING TIME: OVERNIGHT

SMOKE TIME: 60 MINUTES

PREFERRED WOOD: HICKORY

INGREDIENTS

- ½ a cup + 2 teaspoons of lemon pepper
- 1 quart of cold water
- 1 fresh whole chicken

Cooking Directions

1. Take a ½ a cup of lemon pepper and add them to the re-sealable bag

2. Add 1 quart of water and stir well

3. Rinse the chicken and add brine

4. Chill for 8 hours

5. Pre-heat an oil-free fryer to 350 degrees Fahrenheit and add the contents of the bag, making sure to sprinkle 2 teaspoons of lemon pepper on top

6. Cook for a while

7. Prepare your smokers water pan accordingly and pre-heated the smoker to 165 degrees Fahrenheit/121 degree Celsius

8. Smoke and cook for 60 minutes more until the internal temperature reaches 165 degrees Fahrenheit/73 degree Celsius making sure to replace the woods after every 15 minutes

9. Enjoy!

STUFFED PEPPERS WITH CHICKEN AND RICE

It's magical to think what you can do with pieces of peppers! Just look at these bad boys. Peppers stuffed with rice and chicken, who would've ever thought of that?

SERVING: 4

PREP TIME: 20 MINUTES

SMOKE TIME: 50 MINUTES

PREFERRED WOOD: HICKORY

INGREDIENTS

- 4 pieces of bell pepper
- ½ of a small onion finely minced up
- 2 cups of cooked rice
- 1 can of Rotel tomatoes and green chile
- 2 cups of shredded cooked chicken
- 2 tablespoon of chopped fresh cilantro
- Salt as needed
- Black pepper as needed

COOKING DIRECTIONS

1. Prepare your smoker water according to instructions and preheat your smoker to 275 degrees Fahrenheit/135 degree Celsius

2. Fill up a medium-sized bowl and add 3-4 handful of wood chips and allow them to soak

3. Slice up ½ inch off the top of your bell pepper and discard the stem

4. Scoop out the membrane and seeds and set the pepper on the side

5. Take a large sized bowl and add onion, rice, cilantro, Rotel chicken, and mix them well

6. Mince the pepper tops and add them to the mixture

7. Season with some salt and pepper

8. Spoon the mixture into your peppers

9. Transfer them to your smoker rack and add chips to your loading bay, making sure to keep adding more chips after every 30 minutes

10. Smoke for 50 minutes until the peppers are soft

11. Serve and enjoy!

HOLIDAY SPECIAL TURKEY BREAST

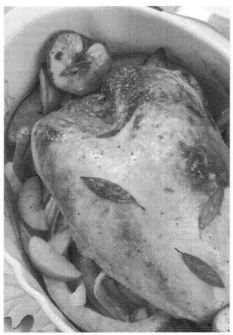

Are turkeys only for holidays? Not really! With this recipe, you can enjoy a nice Turkey meal every single day of the year!

SERVING: 8

PREP TIME: 15 MINUTES

SMOKE TIME: 3 AND A ½ TO 4 AND A ½ HOUR

PREFERRED WOOD: APPLE, HICKORY OR CHERRY

INGREDIENTS

- 6-8 pound of bone-in whole turkey breast
- ½ a cup of soft butter
- ¼ cup of chopped fresh herbs
- 1 tablespoon of minced garlic
- 1 tablespoon of coarse kosher salt
- 1 teaspoon of black pepper

Cooking Directions

1. Prepare the water pan of your smoker accordingly

2. Pre-heat your smoker to 250 degrees Fahrenheit/121 degree celsius

3. Fill a medium-sized bowl with water and add 3-4 handfuls of your preferred chips and allow them to soak

4. Remove the giblets from your turkey and rinse the turkey well

5. Pat it dry

6. Take a medium-sized bowl and add butter alongside the rest of the ingredients

7. Stir them well using a fork

8. Rub the breast with the mixture on all sides

9. Add the mixture under loose skin for added flavor

10. Set your breast on the smoker rack with the skin side facing up and add a handful of your wood in the loading bay (making sure to keep adding more chips every 30 minutes)

11. Smoke for 3 and a ½ to 4 and a ½ hour until the internal temperature reaches 165 degrees Fahrenheit/73 degree Celsius

12. Remove the turkey from the smoker and allow it to cool under a foil tent for 30 minutes

13. Slice and serve!

Chapter 2: Fish and Seafood Recipes

Cumin and Lime Shrimp Delight

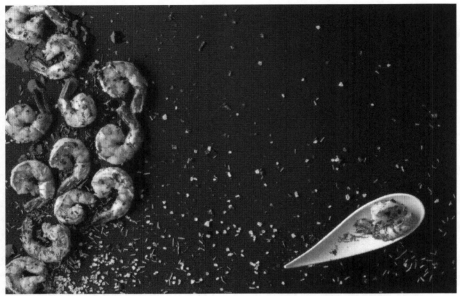

A very fancy cuisine made for the Royals. This shrimp meal is light on the fat but heavy on the delightful flavors.

Serving: 4

Prep Time: 20 minutes

Smoke Time: 30 minutes

Preferred Wood: Beech

Ingredients

- 1 pound of raw shrimp (peeled and deveined)
- 8 wooden skewers
- 2 teaspoon of coarse kosher salt
- 2 teaspoon of ground cumin
- 2 teaspoon of garlic powder
- Zest of 3 limes

COOKING DIRECTIONS

1. Prepare the water pan of your smoker accordingly

2. Pre-heat your smoker to 275 degrees Fahrenheit/135 degree Celsius

3. Fill a medium-sized bowl with water and add 3-4 handfuls of hickory chips and allow them to soak

4. Thread 5-6 shrimp onto each of the skewer

5. Take a small sized bowl and add salt, cumin, lime zest, garlic powder

6. Rub the mix over your shrimp

7. Prepare a 9x13 inch foil pan by poking a dozen holes using fork on the bottom

8. Grease it up with cooking spray

9. Arrange the skewers in the pan and place it in your smoker

10. Add chips to the loading bay and keep adding them after every 15 minutes

11. Smoke for 30 minutes until the shrimps are done

12. Enjoy!

THE CLASSICAL SEAFOOD SCAMPI

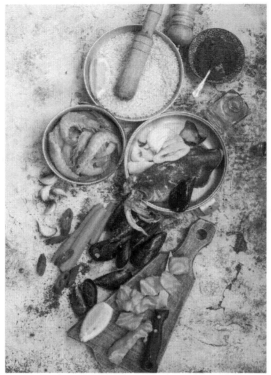

A mishmash of a few different types of fish makes this smoked scampi something to remember. Go with this recipe if you want to have something more than just a meal, this is nothing short of an experience.

SERVING: 4

PREP TIME: 20 MINUTES

SMOKE TIME: 30-40 MINUTES

PREFERRED WOOD: BEECH

INGREDIENTS

- 1 cup of butter
- 8-10 cloves of finely minced garlic
- ½ a pound of fresh scallops
- ½ a pound of crab meat

- ½ a pound of raw shrimp
- Pinch of salt
- 1 pound of dry spaghetti
- 3 tablespoon of finely chopped fresh parsley

COOKING DIRECTIONS

1. Prepare the water pan of your smoker accordingly

2. Pre-heat your smoker to 275 degrees Fahrenheit/135 degree Celsius

3. Fill a medium-sized bowl with water and add 3-4 handfuls of hickory chips and allow them to soak

4. Take a small sized saucepan and place it over medium heat

5. Add butter and allow it to melt

6. Add garlic and warm it

7. Pour the butter into an 8x12 inch foil pan

8. Add garlic and just a pinch of salt and stir well to combine

9. Add the fresh seafood as well and stir to coat them well

10. Add the pan to your smoker and load up the bay with wood chips

11. Make sure to keep adding more chips after every 15 minutes

12. Smoke for 40 minutes until the seafood is cooked

13. Once done, serve with some pasta!

Seasoned Crab Legs

Some people are afraid of smoking crabs, are you one of them? You are missing out on one of the most delicious smoked fish ever!

SERVING: 4

PREP TIME: 5 MINUTES

SMOKE TIME: 20 MINUTES

PREFERRED WOOD: BEECH

INGREDIENTS

- 1 and a /12 pound of pre-cooked crab legs
- ¼ cup of old bay seasoning
- Melted butter for added flavor

COOKING DIRECTIONS

1. Prepare the water pan of your smoker accordingly

2. Pre-heat your smoker to 275 degrees Fahrenheit/135 degree Celsius

3. Fill a medium-sized bowl with water and add 3-4 handfuls of hickory chips and allow them to soak

4. Add the crab leg to a 2-gallon zip bag and add the Old Bay seasoning

5. Seal up completely and shake well to allow the crab legs to coat up

6. Allow it to sit for 10 minutes

7. Transfer the legs to a grill basket and place it in your smoker

8. Add chips to your loading bay and keep adding after every 20 minutes

SPICY CAJUN SALMON BLT

The classical woodman's rough and tough BLT. Nothing more to say about this! This one is for the more adventurous ones.

SERVING: 4

PREP TIME: 20 MINUTES

SMOKE TIME: 30-40 MINUTES

PREFERRED WOOD: BEECH

INGREDIENTS

- 1 tablespoon of onion powder
- 1 tablespoon of paprika
- 2 teaspoon of dried thyme
- 2 teaspoon of garlic powder
- 2 teaspoon of dried oregano
- 1 teaspoon of coarse kosher salt
- ½ a teaspoon of cayenne pepper
- ½ a teaspoon of black pepper
- 1/3 cup of mayonnaise
- 1/3 cup of Smoked Walnut Pesto (recipe in this book)
- 4 pieces of salmon fillets (4-6 ounce each)
- 2 tablespoon of olive oil

- 4 hearty rolls such as Ciabatta
- 8 slices of hickory – smoked bacon, cooked
- 4 Romaine lettuce leaves
- 4 tomato slices

COOKING DIRECTIONS

1. Prepare the water pan of your smoker accordingly

2. Pre-heat your smoker to 275 degrees Fahrenheit/135 degree Celsius

3. Fill a medium-sized bowl with water and add 3-4 handfuls of woods and allow them to soak

4. Take a small sized bowl and add onion powder, thyme, paprika, oregano, black pepper, salt, and mix well

5. Take a separate bowl and add mayonnaise walnut pesto and chill

6. Pat your salmon dry using paper towels

7. Rub each of the fillets with drizzles of olive oil and the dry seasoning mix

8. Store any leftover mix in the fridge

9. Prepare a foil pan and poke dozens of small holes using a knife

10. Spray it with cooking spray

11. Lay the fish in the pan and place it in the smoker

12. Add a small handful of chips in the loading bay and keep adding chips after every 15 minutes

13. Smoke the fish for 30-40 minutes until the thickest part of the fish shows 145 degrees Fahrenheit/62 Degree Celsius

14. Add the smoked salmon pieces on heart roll and spread pesto mayo

15. Top up with lettuce leaf, bacon, tomato slice and enjoy!

GENTLY SMOKED SABLEFISH

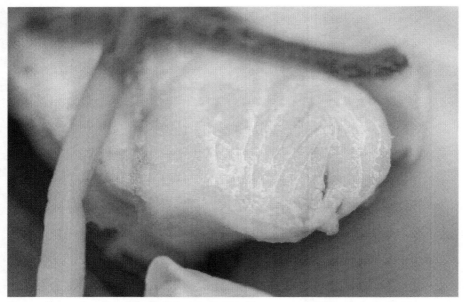

Ever heard of sablefish? No? Well, you really should! Because this will give you something amazing!

SERVING: 6

PREP TIME: 15 MINUTES

MARINADE TIME: 180 MINUTES

SMOKE TIME: 3 HOURS

PREFERRED WOOD: ALDER

INGREDIENTS

- 2-3 pounds of sablefish fillets
- 1 cup of kosher salts
- ¼ cup of sugar
- 2 tablespoon of garlic powder
- Honey for glazing
- Sweet paprika for dusting

COOKING DIRECTIONS

1. Take a bowl and add garlic powder, salt, and sugar
2. Take a plastic tub and add the mix
3. Cut up the fish into fillets and add them to the tub
4. Massage the mix into the fish carefully and place them skin side up on the salt mix
5. Cover and allow it to chill for about 3-4 hours
6. Remove the fish and place it in cold water for a while
7. Pat, it dry using a kitchen towel
8. Prepare the water pan of your smoker accordingly
9. Pre-heat your smoker to 160 degrees Fahrenheit/71 degree Celsius
10. Fill a medium-sized bowl with water and add 3-4 handfuls of woods and allow them to soak
11. Smoke for 2-3 hours making sure to keep basting the fish with honey every hour
12. Once done, allow the fish to cool in a cooling rack
13. Baste with more honey
14. Allow it to cool for an hour
15. Dust with some paprika and wait for 30 minutes
16. Serve and enjoy!

FIERCELY SMOKED TROUT

If your husband is a fisherman, then simply show him this recipe and it will instantly blow him away! A friendly way to bring a smile on the face of a fisherman.

SERVING: 4

PREP TIME: 5 MINUTES

MARINATE TIME: OVERNIGHT

SMOKE TIME: 3-4 HOURS

PREFERRED WOOD: APPLE CHIPS

INGREDIENTS

- 4-6 trout fillets
- 2 cups of water
- ¼ cup of soy sauce
- ¼ cup of teriyaki sauce
- ½ a tablespoon of salt
- 1 teaspoon of lemon pepper
- Garlic salt as needed
- Dill seed as needed

COOKING DIRECTIONS

1. Take a small sized container and add water, teriyaki sauce, soy sauce and salt alongside the other ingredients that you prefer

2. Place the fillets into your marinade and allow it to soak overnight

3. Pre-heat your smoker to 225 degrees Fahrenheit/107 degree Celsius

4. Fill a medium-sized bowl with water and add 3-4 handfuls of hickory chips and allow them to soak

5. Add soaked chips to the loading bay and keep adding more chips after every 30 minutes

6. Smoke the fillets for 3-4 hours until they are nice and flaky

7. Enjoy!

Brown Sugar Salmon

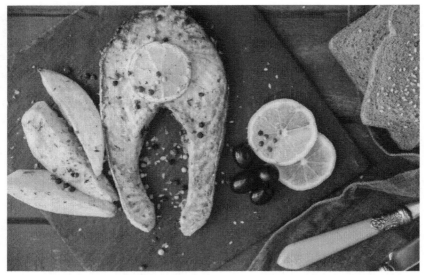

No seafood recipe section would be complete without a few salmon recipes, right? This one is a classic, to say the least with its juicy flavor and sugary sweetness.

SERVING: 4

PREP TIME: 15 MINUTES

SMOKE TIME: 1 TO 1 AND A ½ HOUR

PREFERRED WOOD: MAPLE

INGREDIENTS

- 4 salmon fillets skin removed
- 2 tablespoon of light brown sugar
- ½ a teaspoon of coarse kosher salt
- ½ a teaspoon of black pepper
- Zest of 1 large lemon
- 1 tablespoon of chopped fresh dill
- ¼ cup of real maple syrup
- ¼ cup of yellow mustard

COOKING DIRECTIONS

1. Prepare the water pan of your smoker accordingly

2. Pre-heat your smoker to 225 degrees Fahrenheit/107 degree Celsius

3. Fill a medium-sized bowl with water and add 3-4 handfuls of hickory chips and allow them to soak

4. Check your salmon for any bone and cut them out

5. Take a small bowl and add brown sugar, pepper, and salt

6. Rub the salmon with the mixture (top and sides)

7. Transfer the fillet to a large piece of parchment paper and place them on your smoker

8. Add soaked chips to the loading bay and keep adding more chips after every 30 minutes

9. Allow the salmon to smoke for 1 to 1 and a ½ hour until the internal temperature reaches 145 degree Fahrenheit/62 degree Celsius

10. Take small sized bowl and add lemon juice, zest, maple syrup, dill, mustard and whisk well

11. Brush your salmon with the glaze after every 30 minutes while it is being smoked

12. Serve and enjoy!

SMOKED TUNA

If your family demands a meal of Tuna, then this is what you need! Simply slice up the tuna steak and smoke it up following this recipe. This is a recipe to die for!

SERVING: 4

PREP TIME: 10 MINUTES

SMOKE TIME: 7 HOURS

PREFERRED WOOD: APPLE

INGREDIENTS

- 4 pieces of tuna steak 1 inch thick
- 1 and a 1/8 cup of sugar
- 3/8 cup of salt
- 1 teaspoon of pepper
- ¼ teaspoon of garlic
- ¼ teaspoon of Prague powder
- 1 cup of honey
- 1 gallon of water

COOKING DIRECTIONS

1. Mix all of the above-mentioned ingredients well until they are fully dissolved in water

2. Prepare the water pan of your smoker accordingly

3. Pre-heat your smoker to 140 degrees Fahrenheit/60 degree Celsius

4. Add the fillets and smoke them for 7 hours

5. Once done, enjoy!

CHAPTER 3: PORK RECIPES

BUTTERY BROWN SMOKED PORK

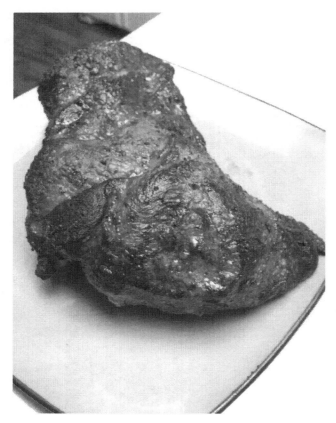

SERVING: 10
PREP TIME: 45 MINUTES
SMOKE TIME: 10 HOURS
PREFERRED WOOD: HICKORY WOODS

INGREDIENTS

- 5 pounds of Pork butt
- Apple cider vinegar – ¾ quarts
- Salt – 4 tablespoons
- Palm sugar – 4 tablespoons

- Black pepper – 4 tablespoons
- Cayenne pepper – 2 ½ tablespoons
- Butter – ½ cup
- Water – 1 quart

COOKING DIRECTIONS

1. Place all of the rub mixture in a pan then bring to boil.

2. Once it is boiled, remove from heat then let it cool.

3. When the spice mixture is cool, divide the mixture into halves.

4. Place the pork but in a container then pour half of the spice mixture over the pork.

5. Cover the container with the lid then refrigerate the pork overnight.

6. Preheat an electric smoker to 250 degrees Fahrenheit/120 degree Celsius

7. Once the electric smoker has reached the desired temperature take the spiced pork out from the container then place on the electric smoker's rack.

8. Smoke the pork butt for 4 hours. Brush the pork with the remaining spice mixture every 30 minutes.

9. After 4 hours, take the pork butt out from the smoker then place in a disposable aluminum pan.

10. Pour the remaining mixture over the pork then cover the pan with aluminum foil.

11. Return the pork butt back to the smoker then smoke for another 2 hours.

12. After 2 hours, remove the pan from the smoker then let it cool.

13. Once the pan is cool, uncover it and transfer the pork to a serving dish.

14. Serve and enjoy.

TENDERLOIN SLIDERS OF PORK

No beach party is complete without tiny and cute sliders right? And it makes the deal even sweeter if the sliders are made from pork tenderloins! The subtlety of the softness is just magical here.

SERVING: 4

PREP TIME: 10 MINUTES

SMOKE TIME: 120 MINUTES

PREFERRED WOOD: HICKORY WOODS

INGREDIENTS

- 1 piece of Pork Tenderloin
- Sea salt as needed
- Fresh ground pepper
- Garlic salt
- 1 pack of slider buns
- Coleslaw
- Hamburger dill pickles

COOKING DIRECTIONS

1. Prepare the water pan of your smoker accordingly

2. Pre-heat your smoker to 225 degrees Fahrenheit/107 degree Celsius

3. Fill a medium-sized bowl with water and add 3-4 handfuls of woods and allow them to soak

4. Season the tenderloin with black pepper, sea salt, garlic salt

5. Smoke them unwrapped for 90 minutes

6. Remove and wrap them up in aluminum foil

7. Place them in the smoker and smoke for another 30 minutes until the temperature reaches 165 degrees Fahrenheit/73 degree Celsius

8. Once done, slice them up into ¼ to 3/8 inch medallions

9. Place them on the slider buns

10. Top up with pickle and Coleslaw

11. Enjoy!

BABY BACK RIBS

These baby back ribs are dipped in brown sugar and special "Montreal" seasoning. Curious? You should be!

SERVING: 4

PREP TIME: 10 MINUTES

STAND TIME: 30 MINUTES

SMOKE TIME: 5 HOURS

PREFERRED WOOD: HICKORY WOODS

INGREDIENTS

- 2 full racks of ribs
- 2 bags of brown sugar
- 1 handful of nature seasoning
- 1 handful of Montreal seasoning
- 1 small bottle of apple juice

COOKING DIRECTIONS

1. Prepare the water pan of your smoker accordingly

2. Pre-heat your smoker to 220 degrees Fahrenheit/104 degree Celsius

3. Fill a medium-sized bowl with water and add 3-4 handfuls of woods and allow them to soak

4. Take a bowl and add the rub seasoning by mixing all of the spices

5. Apply the dry rub all over the ribs and allow them to sit for 30 minutes

6. Place the ribs in your smoker and cook for 3 hours

7. After 3 hours, remove the ribs and wrap them in heavy duty aluminum foil

8. Return to smoker and cook for 1 and a ½ hour until the internal temperature reaches 160 degrees Fahrenheit/71 degree Celsius

PORK BELLY

SERVING: 10
PREP TIME: 10 MINUTES
STAND TIME: 30 MINUTES
SMOKE TIME: 8 HOURS
PREFERRED WOOD: HICKORY WOODS

INGREDIENTS

- Pork belly 5 pounds

FOR RUB

- Dijon mustard – 2 cups
- Orange juice – 2 cups
- Orange zest – 1 teaspoon
- 5 kefir lime leaves
- Pepper – 1 ½ teaspoons
- Salt – 1 teaspoon
- Barbecue sauce – ¾ cup

For Glaze

- Raw honey – ¼ cup
- Orange juice – ½ cup

Cooking Directions

1. Mix the rub ingredients in a bowl then stir well.

2. Rub the pork belly with the spice mixture then let it sit for an hour.

3. Preheat an electric smoker to 225 degrees Fahrenheit /107 degree Celsius

4. Once the electric smoker has reached the desired temperature, place the spiced pork belly on the smoker's rack.

5. Smoke the pork belly for 8 hours and add more wood chips if it is needed.

6. Combine raw honey with orange juice and stir well.

7. Brush the pork belly once every hour with the honey and orange juice mixture.

8. Once it is done or the internal temperature has reached 165 degrees Fahrenheit /74 degree Celsius, take the pork belly out from the smoker and place on a flat surface. Let it cool.

9. Cut the smoked pork belly into medium cubes then place on a serving dish.

10. Serve and enjoy.

INDIAN PORK AND SPICES

A pork meal dipped mysterious spices from India! It's mesmerizing, to say the least.

SERVING: 2 CUPS

PREP TIME: 20 MINUTES

CHILL TIME: 12-24 HOURS

SMOKE TIME: 90 MINUTES

PREFERRED WOOD: PECAN WOODS

INGREDIENTS

- 4 pieces of star anise
- 1 teaspoon of cumin
- 1 teaspoon of coriander
- ½ a teaspoon of cardamom seeds
- ½ a teaspoon of black peppercorns
- 1 teaspoon of turmeric
- ½ a teaspoon of ground red chile
- 1 teaspoon of salt
- 4 tablespoon of canola oil
- 6-8 pound of pork roast

COOKING DIRECTIONS

1. Take a blender and add the first 5 listed spices and grind them

2. Add the remaining three spices and grind

3. Transfer the mix alongside 4 tablespoons of canola oil to a bowl

4. Cover the pork roast with the mixture thoroughly

5. Wrap up the plastic wrap and allow it to chill for 12-24 hours

6. Prepare the water pan of your smoker accordingly

7. Pre-heat your smoker to 225 degrees Fahrenheit/107 degree Celsius

8. Fill a medium-sized bowl with water and add 3-4 handfuls of woods and allow them to soak

9. Smoke until the internal temperature of the roast is at 160 degrees Fahrenheit / 71 degree Celsius

10. Once done, let it rest for 20-30 minutes wrapped in foil

11. Enjoy!

CHAPTER 4: BEEF RECIPES

HOMEMADE ROAST OF BEEF AND A RUMP

When talking about smoked Beef, the first thing that comes to mind is usually Brisket! However, you should know that there is a very affordable yet unknown option known as the Rump! This recipe will give you a very clean and mean Rump for the ages!

SERVING: 4

PREP TIME: 20 MINUTES

SMOKE TIME: 3-4 HOURS

PREFERRED WOOD: HICKORY

INGREDIENTS

FOR RECIPE

- 3 pound of Beef Rump Roast
- 2 cups of beef broth
- Yellow mustard

FOR RUB

- 1 tablespoon of cumin
- 1 tablespoon of paprika
- 1 tablespoon of granulated garlic

- 1 tablespoon of granulated onion
- 1 tablespoon of chili powder
- 1 tablespoon of brown sugar
- 2 tablespoon of kosher salt
- 1 teaspoon of cayenne pepper
- 1 teaspoon of black pepper
- 1 teaspoon of white pepper

COOKING DIRECTIONS

1. Take a small sized bowl and add all of the ingredients for the rub

2. Mix well

3. Season the roast generously with the rub

4. Take a roasting pan and pour broth

5. Place the roast in the pan, making sure that the fatty side is facing up

6. Pre-heat your smoker to 225 degrees Fahrenheit/107 degree Celsius

7. Fill a medium-sized bowl with water and add 3-4 handfuls of hickory chips and allow them to soak

8. Place the pan (uncovered) with the roast and smoke for about 3 hours

9. Keep smoking until the internal part of the meat reaches 135 degrees Fahrenheit/ 57 degree Celsius for a medium doneness

10. Add some chopped up veggies, onion, carrots, and celery if you need

11. Once the meat lamb has reached the desired temperature, remove it from the smoker and carefully wrap it with an aluminum foil

12. Allow it to rest for about 10 minutes

13. Slice it up and enjoy!

51

BUMMED MOUTH-MELTING BURNT ENDS

This is perhaps the only time when burning up your meal will get your praise and adulations! These burnt ends will not only melt in your mouth but will give you a taste a haven!

SERVING: 4

PREP TIME: 10 MINUTES

SMOKE TIME: 3 HOURS

PREFERRED WOOD: HICKORY

INGREDIENTS

- 3 pound of Chuck Roast
- Your preferred dry rub
- Your preferred BBQ Sauce

Cooking Directions

1. Rub the chuck roast all with the dry rub all over

2. Prepare the water pan of your smoker accordingly

3. Pre-heat your smoker to 225 degrees Fahrenheit/107 degree Celsius

4. Fill a medium-sized bowl with water and add 3-4 handfuls of hickory chips and allow them to soak

5. Smoke the meat for 1 and ½ -2 hours until the internal temperature reaches 185 degrees Fahrenheit/ 85 degree Celsius making sure to keep adding more woods after every 30 minutes

6. Allow it to rest for 30 minutes and cube it using sharp knife

7. Add foil pan and enough BBQ to toss the meat well and coat them up

8. Sprinkle with some rub

9. Smoke for another 1 and a ½ hour at 250 degrees Fahrenheit/121 degree Celsius

10. Enjoy once done!

TRADITIONAL BRISKET

If you are familiar with Big Bang Theory, then you must know how much Howard loves Briskets right? Well, this is your chance to experience his mother's authentic brisket recipe! Comes packed with motherly love.

SERVING: 4

PREP TIME: 10 MINUTES

MARINADE TIME: 12 HOURS

SMOKE TIME: 15 HOURS

PREFERRED WOOD: OAK

INGREDIENTS

- 1 pack of brisket split between flat and point
- 1 bottle of your favorite BBQ beef rub
- 3-6 ounce of spicy brown mustard
- Apple juice as needed for basting and bathing
- Beer for cooking and bathing

COOKING DIRECTIONS

1. Trim the brisket well to separate the flat from the point

2. Trim the fat from the separate pieces top ¼ inch

3. Slather the meat well with the spicy brown mustard

4. Rub the meat with rub

5. Allow it to marinade (wrapped up tightly) for 8-12 hours

6. Prepare the water pan of your smoker accordingly

7. Pre-heat your smoker to 230 degrees Fahrenheit/110 degree Celsius

8. Fill a medium-sized bowl with water and add 3-4 handfuls of wood chips and allow them to soak

9. Add the woods to your loading bay

10. Smoke for about 13-15 hours, making sure to add more chips after every 30 minutes until internal temperature reaches 165 degrees Fahrenheit/ 73 degree Celsius. Make sure to keep spritzing it with apple juice after every 2 hours

11. Foil the meat with the last spritz of apple juice and keep smoking until the internal temperature reaches 195 degrees Fahrenheit/ 90 degree Celsius

12. Enjoy!

PRIME ULTRA RIB

The smaller cuts aren't just doing it for you any more right? Behold the ultimate meal for any beef lover! The supreme prime rib! Be sure to treat this with respect.

SERVING: 8

PREP TIME: 10 MINUTES

SMOKE TIME: 4-6 HOURS

PREFERRED WOOD: HICKORY

INGREDIENTS

- 4 chopped garlic cloves
- 2 tablespoon of kosher salt
- 1 tablespoon of freshly ground black pepper
- 1 tablespoon of dried thyme
- 1 prime roast boned (4-6 pounds)

COOKING DIRECTIONS

1. Prepare the water pan of your smoker accordingly

2. Pre-heat your smoker to 250 degrees Fahrenheit/121 degree Celsius

3. Fill a medium-sized bowl with water and add 3-4 handfuls of wood chips and allow them to soak

4. Add the woods to your loading bay

5. Take a bowl and add garlic, pepper, salt, thyme

6. Coat the prime rib evenly with the seasoning

7. Smoke for about 4-6 hours for medium-rare, making sure to add more chips after every 30 minutes until

8. Foil the meat with the last spritz of apple juice and keep smoking until the internal temperature reaches 195 degrees Fahrenheit/ 90 degree Celsius

9. Once the cooking is done, remove the rib and cover It up with aluminum foil

10. Allow it to rest for 15-20 minutes

11. Slice it up and serve!

BEEF FILLETS

Now here's a classic. Nothing too fancy here, just a plain good old smoked up beef fillet ready to be served! Yum

SERVING: 4

PREP TIME: 10 MINUTES

CHILL TIME: 4 HOURS

SMOKE TIME: 60 MINUTES

PREFERRED WOOD: CHERRY CHIPS

INGREDIENTS

- Whole beef Tenderloin sliced up into 1 and a ½ inch thick fillets
- Coarse sea salt as needed
- Freshly ground black pepper as needed
- Garlic pepper as needed

Cooking Directions

1. Season the fillets with sea salt, garlic powder, pepper on both sides

2. Add them to a sheet pan and cover

3. Allow them to chill for 4 hours in the fridge

4. Remove the fillets from the fridge and allow them to rest for 30-45 minutes

5. Prepare the water pan of your smoker accordingly

6. Pre-heat your smoker to 275 degrees Fahrenheit/135 degree Celsius

7. Fill a medium-sized bowl with water and add 3-4 handfuls of wood chips and allow them to soak

8. Add the woods to your loading bay

9. Smoke for 60 minutes, making sure to add more chips after every 30 minutes

10. Take them out at the 1-hour mark for medium rare

11. Allow to rest and enjoy!

12. Enjoy!

CORNED BEEF ALONGSIDE ONION AND POTATOES

Corned beef is a very well-known meal all around the world! If you are interested in making one, just go ahead and try out this special one! The potatoes and onions will give you a very interesting blend of flavors that just might make this your next favorite meal.

SERVING: 8

PREP TIME: 15 MINUTES

SMOKE TIME: 4-5 HOURS

PREFERRED WOOD: HICKORY

INGREDIENTS

- 1 corned beef brisket with spice packet
- 1 can of Coca-Cola
- 6 divided garlic cloves
- 5 pieces of bay leaves
- 1 and a ½ pound of tiny gold potatoes
- 1 large sized coarsely chopped onion
- 2 tablespoon of extra virgin olive oil
- 2 teaspoon of sea salt

Cooking Directions

1. Discard the liquid in the brisket bag

2. Add the brisket in a deep 12-inch square disposable aluminum foil and pour Coca-Cola over

3. Add spice packet

4. Add 2 garlic cloves alongside 1 tablespoon of pickling spice

5. Cover with aluminum foil and refrigerate for about 3 hours

6. Prepare the water pan of your smoker accordingly by adding bay leaves, 3 tablespoon of pickling spice and 4 garlic cloves

7. Wash the potatoes carefully and place them on a disposable aluminum foil

8. Drizzle them with oil and salt

9. Cover with foil

10. Pre-heat your smoker to 225 degrees Fahrenheit/107 degree Celsius

11. Smoke the brisket for about 4 and a ½ hour to 5 hours until the internal temperature reaches 150 degrees Fahrenheit/65 degree Celsius. Make sure to keep adding more woods after everything 30 minutes

12. Add the foil with potatoes during the final hour of brisket smoking

13. Remove the brisket and unwrap foil

14. Return brisket and smoke for another 30 minutes

15. Remove the brisket alongside potatoes

16. Slice up brisket and serve with the smoked potatoes and onions.

CHAPTER 5: LAMB RECIPES

THE IRISH SMOKED LAMB

This is a very simple albeit "Lucky" lamb dish that can be prepped with ease using your electric smoker. Simply follow the ingredients and you will end up with a very juicy and succulent smoked lamb that will surely give you the luck of the Irish! The next time face a wall in your life, just cook and eat this one up! Everything will become clear.

SERVING: 4

PREP TIME: 20 MINUTES

SMOKE TIME: 4 HOURS

PREFERRED WOOD: OAK

INGREDIENTS

FOR LAMB

- 1 boneless lamb leg
- 3 tablespoon of fresh rosemary
- 4 pieces of minced garlic cloves
- 2 tablespoon of black pepper
- 2 tablespoon of kosher salt

FOR POTATOES

- 15 pieces of potatoes
- 1 cup of diced onion
- 1 cup of seeded and diced bell pepper
- 1 tablespoon of salt
- 1 tablespoon of black pepper
- 2 cloves of minced garlic cloves

COOKING DIRECTIONS

1. Take a small sized bowl and add the ingredients for the lamb rub (all except lamb leg)

2. Butterfly your lamb and add half of the ingredients inside

3. Rub the surface of the lamb with remaining rub

4. Close the leg and tie it up with a kitchen tie to secure it well

5. Prepare the water pan of your smoker accordingly

6. Pre-heat your smoker to 225 degrees Fahrenheit/107 degree Celsius

7. Fill a medium-sized bowl with water and add 3-4 handfuls of wood chips and allow them to soak

8. Place it on the upper shelf of your smoker

9. Allow the lamb to smoke

10. After 60 minutes, add potatoes, bell pepper and onion in a sturdy pan

11. Sprinkle minced up garlic, black pepper, and salt over the potatoes

12. Place the pan under the rack with the lamb

13. Allow them to smoke for another 2-2 and a ½ hour

14. Once done, mix both of them and enjoy!

BARBACOA OF LAMB

You have no idea how awesome a Lamb Shoulder Roast can be once it has been dipped and dredged under awesome spicy barbacoa sauce! Don't be alarmed with the steps in this recipe, it's well worth it!

SERVING: 4-8

PREP TIME: 30 MINUTES

SMOKE TIME: 6 HOURS

PREFERRED WOOD: OAK

INGREDIENTS

FOR RUB

- 1 tablespoon of Kosher salt
- 1 tablespoon of ancho chile powder
- 1 tablespoon of guajillo chile powder
- 1 tablespoon of ground cumin
- 2 teaspoon of dried oregano
- 2 teaspoon of onion powder
- 2 teaspoon of garlic powder

- 1 teaspoon of chipotle chili powder
- ¼ teaspoon of ground cloves
- 4 pound of boneless lamb roast tied up (shoulder)

FOR SAUCE

- 4 cups of low sodium chicken stock
- 1 stemmed and seeded ancho chile
- 2 guajillo chiles
- 3 tablespoon of vegetable oil
- ½ a cup of finely chopped white onion
- 4 medium-sized garlic cloves, smashed and peeled
- 1 teaspoon of dried oregano
- 1 teaspoon of ground cumin
- ¼ teaspoon of ground cloves
- ¼ teaspoon of ground cinnamon
- 1/3 cup of apple cider vinegar
- 3 tablespoon of finely chopped chipotle + 1 tablespoon of adobo sauce
- 2 pieces of bay leaves
- ¼ cup of freshly squeezed lime juice from 2 pieces of lime
- Kosher salt as needed

FOR SERVING

- Corn tortillas, cilantro, onion, limes and tomatillo salsa for serving

COOKING DIRECTIONS

1. Prepare the rub by taking a bowl and add mixing all of the ingredients listed under the rub

2. Mix well and season your lamb roast generously with the rub

3. Prepare the water pan of your smoker accordingly

4. Pre-heat your smoker to 250 degrees Fahrenheit/121 degree Celsius

5. Fill a medium-sized bowl with water and add 3-4 handfuls of wood chips and allow them to soak

6. Place the lamb in your smoker directly and allow it to smoke for about 3 hours, making sure to keep adding fresh wood chips after every 30 minutes

7. In the meantime, toast your chilies in a large-sized Dutch oven set to medium heat until they release a nice fragrance, making sure to keep turning them from time to time using a tong

8. Transfer the toasted Chiles to a small-sized saucepan and add 2 cups of your stock

9. Bring the whole mix to a boil over high heat

10. Lower down the heat to low and simmer for about 15 minutes

11. Keep it on the side

12. Add oil and heat it to your Dutch oven over high heat

13. Add onion and garlic and cook for about 10 minutes until they are tender and soft

14. Add oregano, ground cloves, cumin, cinnamon and keep cooking for 30 seconds more until a nice fragrance comes

15. Add 2 cups of extra stock alongside chipotles, vinegar and bring it to a boil again

16. Lower down the heat to medium

17. Simmer for about 20 minutes until the liquid has been halved

18. Transfer the contents of the oven to a blender

19. Add soaked chilies and soaking liquid

20. Puree the whole mixture for about 1 minute

21. Transfer the smoked lamb to your oven

22. Pour the sauce on top alongside bay leaves

23. Lock up the lid of the Dutch oven and keep it there until slightly cracked

24. Transfer to your smoker and keep smoking the lamb for another 2-3 hours until a metal skewer can be penetrated very easily

25. Transfer the lamb to a plate

26. Discard the bay leaves

27. Set your Dutch oven to stovetop mode and cook the sauce over medium-high heat for about 5 minutes

28. Skim any excess

29. Stir in lime juice

30. Untie your smoked lamb roast

31. Pull meat and return it to your sauce and keep it covered for a while to allow the flavors to seep in

32. Allow it to chill overnight if possible

33. Place the shredded lamb meat and sauce in your Dutch oven (setting it to medium heat)

34. Fold the lamb well until it is warmed thoroughly

35. Season with some salt

36. Serve on your corn tortillas, tomatillo, salsa, and cilantro

37. Enjoy!

AMERICAN LAMB LEG WITH TEXAS DRY RUB

A unique recipe that brings you the original American Lamb Recipe and combines the rough and toughness of the cowboys of Texas. Yee-Haw!

SERVING: 4-8

PREP TIME: 30 MINUTES

MARINADE TIME: 8 HOURS

SMOKE TIME: 7-8 HOURS

PREFERRED WOOD: HICKORY

INGREDIENTS

FOR LAMB LEG

- 5-7 pounds of the whole American leg of lamb

FOR DRY RUB

- 1 tablespoon of fresh coriander
- 1 tablespoon of yellow mustard seed
- 1 tablespoon of cumin
- 2 tablespoon of brown sugar
- 2 tablespoon of paprika
- 2 tablespoon of sea salt
- 1 tablespoon of chili powder
- 1 tablespoon of garlic powder
- 1 tablespoon of dried oregano
- 2 teaspoon of fresh ground black pepper

COOKING DIRECTIONS

1. Take a skillet and place it over medium heat

2. Add coriander, cumin and mustard seeds and toast for 2 minutes

3. Use a spice grinder and powder them

4. Add the rest of the dry rub ingredients

5. Generously massage the lamb leg all over and allow it to marinade overnight

6. Prepare the water pan of your smoker accordingly

7. Pre-heat your smoker to 250 degrees Fahrenheit/121 degree Celsius

8. Fill a medium-sized bowl with water and add 3-4 handfuls of wood chips and allow them to soak

9. Smoke for about 7-8 hours making sure to keep adding more chips after every 30 minutes

10. Keep smoking until the internal temperature reaches 190 degrees Fahrenheit/ 87 degree Celsius

11. Remove to a cutting board and slice it up

12. Enjoy!

LAMB RACKS AND PISTACHIOS

If you are looking for something a little bit crunchy! Add some pistachios to the mix, your lamb will no longer be soft! Rather, it will be an amazing treat that resembles a lamb biscuit!

SERVING: 4-8

PREP TIME: 10 MINUTES

MARINADE TIME: 8 HOURS

SMOKE TIME: 1-2 HOURS

PREFERRED WOOD: HICKORY

INGREDIENTS

- 6 pieces of garlic cloves
- ¼ cup of fresh mint leaves
- 2 tablespoon of extra virgin olive oil
- 1 tablespoon of sea salt
- 2 teaspoon of cumin seeds
- 1 teaspoon of fennel seeds
- 1 teaspoon of Coriander seeds
- 1 teaspoon of Black Peppercorns

- 1/3 cup of shelled pistachios
- 1 and a ½ pound of lamb rack
- 2 tablespoon of loose tea leaves
- 2 teaspoon of granulated sugar

COOKING DIRECTIONS

1. Add garlic, olive oil, mint, salt, fennel, cumin, coriander, and black peppercorns to a food processor and pulse them well

2. Add the mix pistachio and mix until coarse

3. Spread the mixture all over the lamb rack and allow it to chill overnight

4. Prepare the water pan of your smoker accordingly

5. Pre-heat your smoker to 375 degrees Fahrenheit/190 degree Celsius

6. Fill a medium-sized bowl with water and add 3-4 handfuls of wood chips and allow them to soak

7. Smoke for about 90-120 minutes

8. Keep smoking until the internal temperature reaches 135 degrees Fahrenheit/ 57 degree Celsius

9. Remove to a cutting board and slice it up

10. Enjoy!

BRAISED LAMB SHANKS

Beautifully prepared Braised and Smoked Lamb Shank! Just don't go poking people with them!

SERVING: 4

PREP TIME: 20 MINUTES

SMOKE TIME: 10 HOURS

PREFERRED WOOD: APPLE

INGREDIENTS

- 2 pieces of lamb shanks
- 1 to 2 cups of water
- ½ a cup of soy sauce
- ½ a cup of rice wine
- ½ a cup of packed dark light brown sugar
- 3 tablespoon of Asian sesame oil
- 4 strips of orange and tangerine zest
- 3 whole star anise
- 2 pieces of cinnamon sticks

COOKING DIRECTIONS

1. Take a sharp knife and pierce the lamb shanks all over about 20 minutes

2. Place the shanks on an aluminum foil

3. Take a bowl and add water, soy sauce, brown sugar, rice wine and sesame oil to the bowl

4. Add orange zest, star anise, and cinnamon stick

5. Pour over the lamb

6. Prepare the water pan of your smoker accordingly

7. Pre-heat your smoker to 225 degrees Fahrenheit/107 degree Celsius

8. Fill a medium-sized bowl with water and add 3-4 handfuls of wood chips and allow them to soak

9. Place the lamb with the braizing liquid in the smoker and smoke until it is dark brown for about 8-10 hours, making sure to turn them after every 30 minutes until the internal temperature reaches 195 degrees Fahrenheit/90 degree Celsius

10. Enjoy!

CHAPTER 6: GAME RECIPES
ONION GRILLED QUAIL

This is another simple Quail recipe that takes a more wild route by adding the flavors of wine and onion!

SERVING: 4

PREP TIME: 10 MINUTES

MARINATE TIME: 2-4 HOURS

SMOKE TIME: 2-3 HOURS

PREFERRED WOOD: APPLE

INGREDIENTS

- 6 pieces of Quail
- 1 cup of dry white wine
- 1 large sized white onion chopped up
- 1 large sized white onion sliced
- 2 tablespoon of olive oil
- ½ a teaspoon of salt
- ½ a teaspoon of peppercorns cracked up
- ½ a teaspoon of crushed garlic

COOKING DIRECTIONS

1. Take a bowl and add all of the ingredients to the bowl except one onion and quail

2. Take a re-sealable bag and add the quail

3. Add the rest of the ingredients and allow them to marinade for 6 hours

4. Slice up the onions thinly into rings

5. Saute the onions until they are lightly browned

6. Prepare the water pan of your smoker accordingly

7. Pre-heat your smoker to 200 degrees Fahrenheit/93 degree Celsius

8. Fill a medium-sized bowl with water and add 3-4 handfuls of Apple chips and allow them to soak

9. Smoke for 2-3 hours making sure to keep adding new chips after every 30-60 minutes until the internal temperature reaches 165 degrees Fahrenheit/ 73 degree Celsius

10. Allow them to rest for 5 minutes

11. Split and enjoy!

BACON WRAPPED UP VENISON TENDERLOIN

And to top off the venison recipes, here's the age-old favorite one! A recipe that wraps up delicious venison medallions within slices of Bacon. Just reading about it starts to make you drool, doesn't it? Just imagine how cool the final product is going to be!

SERVING: 4

PREP TIME: 10 MINUTES

MARINADE TIME: 2 HOURS

SMOKE TIME: 2-3 HOURS

PREFERRED WOOD: APPLE

INGREDIENTS

- 2 pieces of tenderloins
- 6 slices of bacon
- 2 tablespoon of Worcestershire sauce

- 2 tablespoon of water
- 2 tablespoon of vegetable oil
- 1 teaspoon of finely chopped garlic
- 1 teaspoon of salt
- 1 and a ½ teaspoon of black pepper

COOKING DIRECTIONS

1. Cut up the tenderloins into bacon wide sections of about 1 and a ½ inch

2. Cut the bacon in half and wrap them up half slice around the medallions

3. Use a toothpick to secure them in place

4. Take a bowl and add the marinade ingredients and mix them up

5. Allow the medallions to marinate for 2 hours

6. Prepare the water pan of your smoker accordingly

7. Pre-heat your smoker to 140 degrees Fahrenheit/60 degree Celsius

8. Fill a medium-sized bowl with water and add 3-4 handfuls of Apple chips and allow them to soak

9. Smoke for 3-4 hours making sure to keep adding new chips after every 30-60 minutes until the internal temperature is 135 Fahrenheit/57 degree Celsius

10. Enjoy once done!

VENISON BACKSTRAP

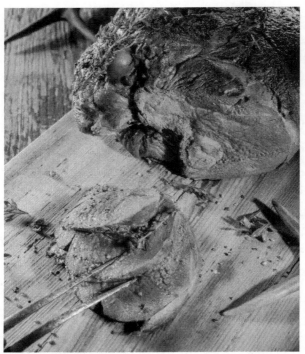

This is the best deer recipe if you want to go for the big game! The Backstrap smoked meal will give you enough meat to re-create the last supper over and over again your tummy is totally full!

SERVING: 4

PREP TIME: 10 MINUTES

SMOKE TIME: 12 HOURS

PREFERRED WOOD: HICKORY

INGREDIENTS

- 1 butterflied venison Backstrap
- 6 slices of bacon
- 2 large sized Yukon Gold potatoes chopped up
- 8 ounce of sliced mushrooms
- 1 and a ½ cup of whole kernel corns

- 1 medium-sized white onion chopped up
- 3 chopped up scallions
- 2 tablespoon of fresh parsley chopped up
- 1 teaspoon of salt
- 1 and a ½ teaspoon of black pepper
- Vegetable oil as needed

COOKING DIRECTIONS

1. Take a pan and place it over medium heat
2. Add bacon and vegetable oil and fry them well
3. Save the grease for later use
4. Add corn and fry them until just starts to brown up
5. Add chopped up yellow onion and mushrooms and keep frying until tender
6. Remove them
7. Add bacon grease and fry potatoes until they are nice and browned
8. Remove them
9. Fry onions until tender
10. Add parsley and cook for another minute
11. Remove heat
12. Take a mixing bowl and add potatoes and mash them
13. Crumble the bacon and add them alongside the other ingredients to the potatoes
14. Season with some salt and pepper
15. Stir well
16. Add the hot filling onto the butterflied loin down the middle
17. Roll up the meat around the filling
18. Skewer with bamboo

19. Coat the outside with vegetable oil and season with some pepper and salt

20. Prepare the water pan of your smoker accordingly

21. Pre-heat your smoker to 230 degrees Fahrenheit/110 degree Celsius

22. Fill a medium-sized bowl with water and add 3-4 handfuls of Hickory chips and allow them to soak

23. Smoke for 12-16 hours making sure to keep adding new chips after every 30-60 minutes

24. Enjoy once done!

THE PERFECT GREEK STYLED QUAIL

The Greek Gods only ate meals that were worthy of their valor! Rest assured, this Green Styled Quail is undoubtedly worthy of the Gods, and you as well! Don't forget to lick your fingers once you are done!

SERVING: 4

PREP TIME: 10 MINUTES

MARINATE TIME: 2-4 HOURS

SMOKE TIME: 2-3 HOURS

PREFERRED WOOD: APPLE

INGREDIENTS

- 6 pieces of Quail
- 3 tablespoon of extra virgin olive oil
- 3 tablespoon of red wine
- 2 tablespoon of lemon juice
- 1 tablespoon of oregano
- ½ a teaspoon of salt
- ¼ teaspoon of black pepper

COOKING DIRECTIONS

1. Take your quail and place it into a gallon sized freezer storage bag

2. Add the remaining ingredients and mix well

3. Pour the marinade into the bag with the quail

4. Coat them well

5. Allow them to marinate for 2 hours or more (max 4 hours)

6. Prepare the water pan of your smoker accordingly

7. Pre-heat your smoker to 200 degrees Fahrenheit/93 degree Celsius

8. Fill a medium-sized bowl with water and add 3-4 handfuls of Hickory chips and allow them to soak

9. Smoke for 2-3 hours making sure to keep adding new chips after every 30-60 minutes until the internal temperature reaches 165 degrees Fahrenheit/ 73 degree Celsius

10. Allow them to rest for 5 minutes

11. Split and enjoy!

BUTTER QUAIL

Quail eggs are very famous all around the world! And just to let you know, Quail birds are also immensely famous as well! Just grab one and smoke Em up! This is a tricky meal, but is an instant smile bringer!

SERVING: 4

PREP TIME: 10 MINUTES

SMOKE TIME: 2-3 HOURS

PREFERRED WOOD: APPLE

INGREDIENTS

- 4 pieces of Quail
- ¼ cup of butter
- 1 tablespoon of light vegetable oil
- ½ a teaspoon of salt
- ½ a teaspoon of coarse ground black pepper

COOKING DIRECTIONS

1. Prepare the water pan of your smoker accordingly

2. Pre-heat your smoker to 200 degrees Fahrenheit/93 degree Celsius

3. Coat up the quail with vegetable oil

4. Fill a medium-sized bowl with water and add 3-4 handfuls of Hickory chips and allow them to soak

5. Smoke for 2-3 hours making sure to keep adding new chips after every 30-60 minutes until the internal temperature reaches 165 degrees Fahrenheit/ 73 degree Celsius

6. Wait until the Quail is cooled

7. Melt the butter in the meantime

8. Brush the Quail with the butter and enjoy!

9. Enjoy once done!

KINKY GOOSE WITH CITRUS THROWN IN

Similar to duck, smoking a goose isn't that difficult. But when you add some citrus into the mix, this Goose becomes a little bit "kinky" to say the least.

SERVING: 6

PREP TIME: 10 MINUTES

MARINADE TIME: 6 HOURS

SMOKE TIME: 40 MINUTES

PREFERRED WOOD: HICKORY

INGREDIENTS

- ½ a cup of orange juice
- 1/3 cup of olive oil
- 1/3 cup of Dijon mustard
- 1/3 cup of brown sugar
- ¼ cup of soy sauce
- ¼ cup of honey
- 1 tablespoon of dried minced onion
- 1 teaspoon of garlic powder
- 8 goose breast halves
- 1 cup of soaked hickory wood chips

Cooking Directions

1. Take a bowl and whisk in orange juice, olive oil, mustard, soy sauce, honey, sugar onion and garlic powder

2. Mix everything well

3. Add the marinade to the goose and allow it to soak

4. Allow it to chill for 6 hours

5. Prepare the water pan of your smoker accordingly

6. Pre-heat your smoker to 300 degrees Fahrenheit/148 degree Celsius

7. Coat up the quail with vegetable oil

8. Fill a medium-sized bowl with water and add 3-4 handfuls of Hickory chips and allow them to soak

9. Smoke for about 20-30, making sure to keep basting it with marinade for the first 30 minutes

10. Keep smoking until the internal temperature reaches 165 degrees Fahrenheit/ 73 degree Celsius

SMOKED PHEASANT

Pheasants are generally restricted to Asia, so you might have a hard time getting them. However, if you are able to manage them, then they actually make for amazing smoked up dish. However, be warned that this recipe is slightly tricky, but if you able to pull it off, you are guaranteed to fall in love!

SERVING: 4

PREP TIME: 10 MINUTES

MARINADE TIME: 8 HOURS

SMOKE TIME: 3-4

PREFERRED WOOD: APPLE

INGREDIENTS

- 3 whole skinned pheasants
- 3 pieces of skin from leg quarters
- 1 quart of cold water
- 3 tablespoon of kosher salt
- 1 teaspoon of onion powder
- 1 teaspoon of garlic powder
- 1 teaspoon of dried parsley
- ½ a teaspoon of white pepper
- ½ a paprika

COOKING DIRECTIONS

1. Take a bucket and dissolve salted cold water
2. Add the pheasant in the brine and allow it to stay overnight or for 8 hours
3. Rinse them and dry them off using paper towels
4. Take a bowl and mix spices
5. Season the breasts lightly on the surface
6. Wrap them up with the chicken skin and cover it up
7. Secure with toothpicks
8. Dust with spice on top of the skin
9. Prepare the water pan of your smoker accordingly
10. Pre-heat your smoker to 230 degrees Fahrenheit/110 degree Celsius
11. Fill a medium-sized bowl with water and add 3-4 handfuls of Apple chips and allow them to soak
12. Smoke for 3-4 hours making sure to keep adding new chips after every 30-60 minutes until the internal temperature is 165 Fahrenheit/73 degree Celsius
13. Enjoy once done!

CHAPTER 7: SIDES AND VEGGIES

SPICED UP BROCCOLI

If you are having trouble feeding your younglings, then smoke up the broccoli and give it to them. They won't be able to resist it!

SERVING: 4-6

PREP TIME: 15 MINUTES

SMOKE TIME: 60-90 MINUTES

PREFERRED WOOD: HICKORY WOODS

INGREDIENTS

- 1 head of broccoli trimmed up florets
- 2 tablespoon of olive oil
- 2 teaspoon of seasoned
- 1 teaspoon of red pepper flakes

COOKING DIRECTIONS

1. Prepare the water pan of your smoker accordingly

2. Pre-heat your smoker to 230 degrees Fahrenheit/110 degree Celsius

3. Fill a medium-sized bowl with water and add 3-4 handfuls of woods and allow them to soak

4. Place the broccoli in a grill basket in single layer

5. Drizzle them with olive oil and sprinkle with seasoned salt, red pepper

6. Add a few chips into the loading bay and keep repeating until all of the chips after every 20 minutes

7. Smoke for 60-90 minutes

8. Serve and enjoy!

GRADUALLY PREPARED GREEN CHILE CORN BREAD

If you fancy yourself something spicy, then these red wings are the way to go! Subtle in nature, fiery in characteristics!

SERVING: 4-6

PREP TIME: 15 MINUTES

SMOKE TIME: 60-120 MINUTES

PREFERRED WOOD: HICKORY WOODS

INGREDIENTS

- 12 ounce of cornbread mixture
- 4 ounce of diced green chiles (either hot or mild , depending on your preference)
- 2 tablespoon of mayonnaise

COOKING DIRECTIONS

1. Prepare the water pan of your smoker accordingly

2. Pre-heat your smoker to 230 degrees Fahrenheit/110 degree Celsius

3. Fill a medium-sized bowl with water and add 3-4 handfuls of woods and allow them to soak

4. Prepare your cornbread mixture accordingly and stir in mayonnaise and chili into the batter

5. Take an 8-inch iron skillet and grease it with cooking spray

6. Pour the cornbread batter into the skillet and place it in your smoker

7. Add a few chips into the loading bay and keep repeating until all of the chips after every 20 minutes

8. Smoke for 60-90 minutes

9. Serve and enjoy!

MIXED UP VEGETABLE SKEWERS

You've heard of Meat Kabobs! Now be prepared to try out a veggie kabob! Soon you will turn into the light of the party.

SERVING: 10

PREP TIME: 15 MINUTES

SMOKE TIME: 60-90 MINUTES

PREFERRED WOOD: HICKORY WOODS

INGREDIENTS

- 2 slices of zucchini sliced up into ½ inch rounds
- 2 yellow summer squash sliced up into ½ inch rounds
- 1 red onion cut up into large chunks
- 4 bell peppers seeded and cut up into large chunks
- 2 cups of grate tomatoes
- 2 tablespoon of olive oil
- 2 tablespoon of seasoned salt

COOKING DIRECTIONS

1. Prepare the water pan of your smoker accordingly

2. Pre-heat your smoker to 250 degrees Fahrenheit/121 degree Celsius

3. Fill a medium-sized bowl with water and add 3-4 handfuls of woods and allow them to soak

4. Thread the cut vegetables onto your skewer, making sure to alternate the veggies and end with a grape tomato

5. Drizzle olive oil and sprinkle seasoned salt all over

6. Arrange the skewers on the smoker rack

7. Add a few chips into the loading bay and keep repeating until all of the chips after every 20 minutes

8. Smoke for 60-90 minutes . Serve and enjoy!

SMOKY *BBQ* SAUCE

Fancy a homemade BBQ sauce? Well, this is your chance to prove your worth!

SERVING: 2 CUPS

PREP TIME: 20 MINUTES

SMOKE TIME: 90 MINUTES

PREFERRED WOOD: PECAN WOODS

INGREDIENTS

- 2 cups of ketchup
- 1 cup of water
- ½ a cup of vinegar
- ¾ cup of dark brown sugar
- 1 teaspoon of salt
- 1 tablespoon of Worcestershire sauce
- 1 tablespoon of hot sauce
- 1 teaspoon of paprika
- ½ teaspoon of cayenne pepper
- ½ a teaspoon of black pepper
- 2 garlic cloves
- ½ of an onion

Cooking Directions

1. Prepare the water pan of your smoker accordingly

2. Pre-heat your smoker to 215 degrees Fahrenheit/101 degree Celsius

3. Fill a medium-sized bowl with water and add 3-4 handfuls of woods and allow them to soak

4. Take the tomatoes and garlic and place them in a disposable pan and place it to the smoker

5. Add a few chips into the loading bay and keep repeating until all of the chips after every 30 minutes

6. Smoke for 60-90 minutes

7. Transfer the smoked mixture to a medium saucepan and add the rest of the ingredients

8. Place it on top of a medium heat stop and simmer for 5-10 minutes

9. Remove the heat and break everything using an immersion blender

10. Use the sauce immediately or store fridge

VOLCANIC POTATOES OF ERUPTION

These potatoes are nothing short of a Volcano! Oozing with cream and meaty goodness! You just might get addicted to these!

SERVING: 4

PREP TIME: 5 MINUTES

SMOKE TIME: 4 HOURS

PREFERRED WOOD: PECAN WOODS

INGREDIENTS

- 2 pieces of russet potatoes
- ½ a cup of sour cream + extra 2 spoonfuls for garnish
- 1 cup of grated cheddar cheese
- 2 tablespoon of diced green onion
- 4 strips of bacon
- 2-4 strips of bacon to be used as potato filling
- ½ a stick of butter

COOKING DIRECTIONS

1. Prepare the water pan of your smoker accordingly

2. Pre-heat your smoker to 250 degrees Fahrenheit/121 degree Celsius

3. Fill a medium-sized bowl with water and add 3-4 handfuls of woods and allow them to soak

4. Wash the potatoes well and poke them with fork

5. Cover with salt and olive oil

6. Wrap them up in foil and place them on the rack

7. Smoke for 2.5-3 hours

8. Cut the upper part of the potatoes and scoop out the flesh leaving the skin for supporting the filling

9. Take a bowl and add flesh, chopped up bacon, sour cream, butter, and cheese

10. Wrap the potatoes in the bacon and secure with a toothpick

11. Fill up the potatoes with the prepared mixture

12. Add them to your smoker and smoke for another 60 minutes

13. Top with sour cream and enjoy!

SMOKED UP ALMOND

Let end this chapter with a very subtle recipe. Toasted and Smoked Almonds for your crunchy desire!

SERVING: 4

PREP TIME: 5 MINUTES

SMOKE TIME: 10 MINUTES

PREFERRED WOOD: APPLE WOODS

INGREDIENTS

- 2 cups of whole raw almonds
- 1 and a quarter cup of butter
- 1 tablespoon of seasoned salt
- 2 teaspoon of white sugar
- 1 and a half teaspoon of onion powder

COOKING DIRECTIONS

1. Take a skillet and place it over medium heat

2. Add butter and melt it

3. Add almonds and stir for 10 minutes

4. Add salt, onion powder and sugar in a grinder

5. Clean the coffee grinder well and pulverize them until they are powdered

6. Dump the almonds in a colander and strain the melted butter

7. Spread them out on a baking sheet

8. Coat them up with the salt mix

9. Prepare the water pan of your smoker accordingly

10. Pre-heat your smoker to 225 degrees Fahrenheit/107 degree Celsius

11. Fill a medium-sized bowl with water and add 3-4 handfuls of woods and allow them to soak

12. Smoke the nuts until they are nicely toasted

13. Remove and allow them to cool

CHAPTER 8: HOT DOGS AND MEATLOAF

HOT DOGS WITH MUSTARD

These hot dogs will bring a smile to your face (despite being grim) and the mustard will make you go "mamma mia"!

SERVING: 4

PREP TIME: 10 MINUTES

SMOKE TIME: 1 AND ½ HOURS

PREFERRED WOOD: HICKORY

INGREDIENTS

- 6 bratwursts
- 3 tablespoon of vegetable oil
- 1 large sized coarsely diced onion
- 1 large sized coarsely diced green pepper
- 2 minced garlic cloves
- ½ a teaspoon of celery seeds
- ¼ cup of Dijon mustard

COOKING DIRECTIONS

1. Prepare the water pan of your smoker accordingly

2. Pre-heat your smoker to 225 degrees Fahrenheit/107 degree Celsius

3. Fill a medium-sized bowl with water and add 3-4 handfuls of hickory chips and allow them to soak

4. Add 6 bratwursts on the top shelf of your smoker and smoker for 1 and ½ hours until the internal temperature reaches 160 degrees Fahrenheit/71 degree Celsius

5. Take a large sized skillet and add oil

6. Add green pepper and onion and Saute them over medium-low heat

7. Stir well for 10 minutes until they are golden brown

8. Add garlic, celery seeds and keep cooking for 5 minutes

9. Stir in Dijon mustard and cook for another 3 minutes

10. Serve with the meat immediately!

CHEESEBURGER FATTIES

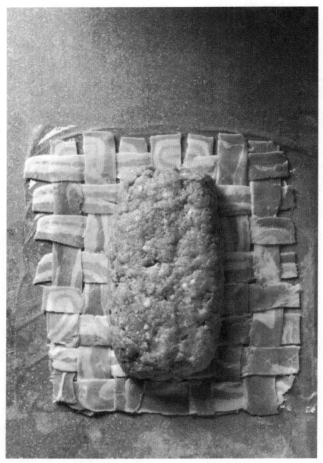

Another "Fatty" recipe that is bound to satisfy anyone who wants the full force of juicy goodness to gush through their bodies and touch every single taste bud with mouth melting meaty addiction. This one is truly for the daring ones, people with heart diseases, be warned!

SERVING: 4

PREP TIME: 10 MINUTES

SMOKE TIME: 2 HOURS

PREFERRED WOOD: HICKORY

INGREDIENTS

- 1 and a ½ pound of ground beef
- 1 pound of bacon
- 1 teaspoon of garlic powder
- 1 teaspoon of salt
- 1 teaspoon of pepper
- 1 teaspoon of onion powder
- 4 tablespoon of A-1 sauce
- ½ a cup of shredded sharp cheddar cheese
- ½ a cup of shredded mozzarella cheese
- ¾ cup chopped up mushrooms
- 10-12 hamburger dill sliced pickles chopped up

COOKING DIRECTIONS

1. Take a bowl and add garlic powder , pepper, salt, onion powder and 2 tablespoons of A-1 sauce alongside ground beef
2. Place the whole mixture into a re-sealable zip bag
3. Make bacon weave
4. Cut up the Ziploc bag down the center and fold the bag
5. Layer 2 tablespoon of A-1 sauce, mushrooms, shredded cheese and pickles in the center of the ground beef blanket
6. Fold the blanket on both sides towards the center and seal it up
7. Seal the ends
8. Place the rolled up beef into the center of your bacon weave
9. Pull both sides and seal the beef roll inside
10. Seal up the ends
11. Prepare the water pan of your smoker accordingly
12. Pre-heat your smoker to 225 degrees Fahrenheit/107 degree Celsius
13. Smoke for 2 hours
14. Enjoy!

FATTY JALAPENOS

Tired of staying healthy? Want to take a break and go wild? These fatties will fill you up to the brim with its juicy and meaty goodness. Let your inner animal out!

SERVING: 4

PREP TIME: 10 MINUTES

SMOKE TIME: 75 MINUTES

PREFERRED WOOD: HICKORY WOODS

INGREDIENTS

- 1 pound of ground beef
- 2 packs of bacon
- Jalapenos
- Cream cheese
- Cheddar cheese
- Salt as needed
- Pepper as needed
- Onion powder as needed
- Garlic powder as needed

Cooking Directions

1. Prepare the water pan of your smoker accordingly

2. Pre-heat your smoker to 225 degrees Fahrenheit/107 degree Celsius

3. Fill a medium-sized bowl with water and add 3-4 handfuls of woods and allow them to soak

4. Blend 1 pound of ground beef with salt, onion powder, pepper and garlic powder

5. Make the individual bacon weaves

6. Quarter the ground beef into 4 individual fatties

7. Flatten the quarters and layer them with cream cheese, jalapenos, and cheddar cheese

8. Roll up the stuffed ground beef and seal them

9. Roll up the stuffed ground beef in bacon weave and transfer them to your smoker

10. Smoke for 75 minutes

11. Slice them up and enjoy!

Very "Yellow" Tailed Dawgz

Be warned that these are not your traditional dogs! In fact, these are the most fascinating and cool 'Dawgz" ever!

SERVING: 4

PREP TIME: 10 MINUTES

SMOKE TIME: 90 MINUTES

PREFERRED WOOD: PECAN WOODS

INGREDIENTS

- 6 pieces of hotdogs
- 1 piece of 750 ml Bottle of Yellow Tail Merlot Wine
- 1 pack of sliced mushrooms
- 8 tablespoon of butter
- 1 teaspoon of garlic powder
- 6 Pepperidge Farm whole wheat hoagie rolls
- 1 pack of shredded Cheddar and Monterey Jack Cheese

COOKING DIRECTIONS

1. Prepare the water pan of your smoker accordingly

2. Pre-heat your smoker to 225 degrees Fahrenheit/107 degree Celsius

3. Fill a medium-sized bowl with water and add 3-4 handfuls of woods and allow them to soak

4. Slice up the mushrooms and place them into a 9x2 round pan

5. Cut up 4 tablespoons of butter on top of your mushrooms

6. Pour ¾ of your Merlot wine

7. Add the pan to the smoker rack (lowest rack) and place 6 hot dogs on the immediate upper rack

8. Smoke for 45 minutes

9. Remove the dogs and cut them lengthwise

10. Add the franks to the pan with mushrooms

11. Lock up the smoker door and smoke for another 45 minutes

12. Brush the inside of the hoagies with 4 tablespoons of melted butter and 1 teaspoon of garlic powder mix

13. Take a clean pan and add the franks in the hoagies

14. Top them up with some smoked mushrooms

15. Garnish with shredded cheese

16. Smoke for a little longer until the cheese has melted

CHAPTER 9: INFORMATION ON SMOKING MEAT

WHAT IS THE PRIMARY DIFFERENCE BETWEEN BARBEQUING A MEAT AND SMOKING IT?

You might not believe it, but there are still people who think that the process of Barbequing and Smoking are the same! So, this is something which you should know about before diving in deeper.

So, whenever you are going to use a traditional BBQ grill, you always put your meat directly on top of the heat source for a brief amount of time which eventually cooks up the meal. Smoking, on the other hand, will require you to combine the heat from your grill as well as the smoke to infuse a delicious smoky texture and flavor to your meat. Smoking usually takes much longer than traditional barbecuing. In most cases, it takes a minimum of 2 hours and a temperature of 100 -120 degrees for the smoke to be properly infused into the meat. Keep in mind that the time and temperature will obviously depend on the type of meat that you are using, and that is why it is suggested that you keep a meat thermometer handy to ensure that your meat is doing fine. Keep in mind that this method of barbecuing is also known as "Low and slow" smoking as well. With that cleared up, you should be aware that there are actually two different ways through which smoking is done.

THE CORE DIFFERENCE BETWEEN COLD AND HOT SMOKING

Depending on the type of grill that you are using, you might be able to get the option to go for a Hot Smoking Method or a Cold Smoking One. The primary fact about these three different cooking techniques which you should keep in mind are as follows:

- **Hot Smoking**: In this technique, the food will use both the heat on your grill and the smoke to prepare your food. This method is most suitable for items such as chicken, lamb, brisket etc.
- **Cold Smoking**: In this method, you are going to smoke your meat at a very low temperature such as 30 degree Celsius, making sure that it doesn't come into the direct contact with the heat. This is mostly used as a means to preserve meat and extend their life on the shelf.
- **Roasting Smoke**: This is also known as Smoke Baking. This process is essentially a combined form of both roasting and baking and can be performed in any type of smoker with a capacity of reaching temperatures above 82 degree Celsius.

THE DIFFERENT TYPES OF WOOD AND THEIR BENEFITS

The Different Types Of Wood	Suitable For
Hickory	Wild game, chicken, pork, cheeses, beef
Pecan	Chicken, pork, lamb, cheeses, fish.
Mesquite	Beef and vegetables
Alder	Swordfish, Salmon, Sturgeon and other types of fishes. Works well with pork and chicken too.
Oak	Beef or briskets
Maple	Vegetable, ham or poultry
Cherry	Game birds, poultry or pork
Apple	Game birds, poultry, beef
Peach	Game birds, poultry or pork
Grape Vines	Beef, chicken or turkey
Wine Barrel Chips	Turkey, beef, chicken or cheeses
Seaweed	Lobster, mussels, crab, shrimp etc.
Herbs or Spices such as rosemary, bay leaves, mint, lemon peels, whole nutmeg etc.	Good for cheeses or vegetables and a small collection of light meats such as fillets or fish steaks.

THE BASIC PREPARATIONS

- Always be prepared to spend the whole day and take as much time as possible to smoke your meat for maximum effect.
- Make sure to obtain the perfect Ribs/Meat for the meal which you are trying to smoke. Do a little bit of research if you need.
- I have already added a list of woods in this book, consult to that list and choose the perfect wood for your meal.
- Make sure to prepare the marinade for each of the meals properly. A great deal of the flavor comes from the rubbing.
- Keep a meat thermometer handy to get the internal temperature when needed.
- Use mittens or tongs to keep yourself safe
- Refrain yourself from using charcoal infused alongside starter fluid as it might bring a very unpleasant odor to your food
- Always make sure to start off with a small amount of wood and keep adding them as you cook.
- Don't be afraid to experiment with different types of wood for newer flavor and experiences.
- Always keep a notebook near you and note jot down whatever you are doing or learning and use them during the future session. This will help you to evolve and move forward.

THE CORE ELEMENTS OF SMOKING!

Smoking is a very indirect method of cooking that relies on a number of different factors to give you the most perfectly cooked meal that you are looking for. Each of these components is very important to the whole process as they all work together to create the meal of your dreams.

- **Time**: Unlike grilling or even Barbequing, smoking takes a really long time and requires a whole lot of patience. It takes time for the smoky flavor to slowly get infused into the meats. Jus to bring things into comparison, it takes an about 8 minutes to fully cook a steak through direct heating, while smoking (indirect heating) will take around 35-40 minutes.

- **Temperature:** When it comes to smoking, the temperature is affected by a lot of different factors that are not only limited to the wind, cold air temperatures but also the cooking wood's dryness. Some smokers work best with large fires that are controlled by the draw of a chimney and restricted airflow through the various vents of the cooking chamber and firebox. While other smokers tend to require smaller fire with fewer coals as well as a completely different combination of the vent and draw controls. However, most smokers are designed to work at temperatures as low as 180 degrees Fahrenheit to as high as 300 degrees Fahrenheit. But the recommend temperature usually falls between 250 degrees Fahrenheit and 275 degrees Fahrenheit.
- **Airflow:** The level of air to which the fire is exposed to greatly determines how your fire will burn and how quickly it will burn the fuel. For instance, if you restrict air flow into the firebox by closing up the available vents, then the fire will burn at a low temperature and vice versa. Typically in smokers, after lighting up the fire, the vents are opened to allow for maximum air flow and is then adjusted throughout the cooking process to make sure that optimum flame is achieved.
- **Insulation:** Insulation is also very important when it comes to smokers as it helps to easily manage the cooking process throughout the whole cooking session. A good insulation allows smokers to efficiently reach the desired temperature instead of waiting for hours upon hours!

Chapter 10: What is an Electric Smoker

In short, electric smokers have paved the way for every American to enjoy the delight of smoked meat from the comfort of your home. These electric smokers are therefore often advertised with the tagline "Set it and Forget It", which easily gives an idea of the core functionality of the appliance. Electric smokers very easily provide the option to smoke meats through an easy-to-use and accessible interface. Since modern Electric Smokers are packed with very intelligent software, the smoker itself monitors the temperature all throughout the smoking process with no human involvement required.All you have to do set it up and allow the smoker to do its magic!

How an Electric Smoker works

Inexpensive Electric Smokers usually use a rheostat that controls the flow of electricity to an internal heating coil (similar to the stove or electric hotplate). A little bit better smokers have three settings such as low, medium and high and the higher end Electric Smokers have amazing thermostats that allow the temperature to be controlled seamlessly. All you have to do is press the buttons of the dials and precisely set the temperature as needed. These smokers are a little bit more expensive but they are well worth it.

The basic features of an Electric Smoker

While Smokers from different brands are bound to have some tricks of their own! There are some features that almost staple to every Electric Smoker out there. Having a good knowledge of these base features will give you a clear idea of what you are going into!

Considerably Spacious: Most Electric Smokers are usually very spacious as to allow you to smoke meat for a large group of people. Generally speaking, the size of the Electric Smoker ranges from 527 square inches to 730 square inches.

Light Weight: Regular charcoal smokers tend to be really bulky and even tough to move! Modern Electric Smokers tend to extremely light in weight, which makes it easier to move and very mobile. An average Electric Smoker usually weighs somewhere around 40-60 pounds. The inner walls of the smokers are made of stainless steel that makes it lightweight and durable.

Construction: Normally, most Electric Smokers are built with durability kept in mind. The design of an Electric Smoker and the ergonomics are often designed with very high quality imported materials that give it a very long lasting and safe build. These appliances are 100% safe for both you and your family.

Chrome Coated Racks: Bigger sized smokers are often divided into 2-4 compartments that are fully plated with high-quality chrome. These racks are very easy to remove and can be used to keep large pieces of meat without making a mess. Even the most basic electric smokers tend to have at least four racks that are chrome coated.

Easily Cleanable: As Electric Smokers are getting more and more advanced, they are also becoming more accessible and easy to use. The Stainless Steel walls mean that you will be able to smoke your meat and veggies with ease and easily clean the smoker afterward.

Safe to Use: Electric Smokers are generally built with much grace and don't pose any harm. However, a degree of caution is always to be kept. As long as you are following the guidelines and maintain proper safety procedures, there's no risk of any kind of accidental burns or electric shocks from a smoker.

THE BASIC STEPS OF USING AN ELECTRIC SMOKER

Now, the good news for all of your smoke aficionados out there is that using an Electric Smoker isn't exactly rocket science! This means anyone will be able to use it, following some very basic and simple guidelines. So it is crucial that you go through this section before starting to smoke your meat. After all, you don't want your expensive cut to be ruined just because of some silly mishap right?

Just follow the basics and you will be fine!

- The first step is to make sure that you always wear safety gloves
- Take out the chips tray and add your wood chips (before smoking begins)
- However, once the smoking has started, you can easily use the side chip tray for adding your chips
- The additional of chips are required to infused the meat with a more smoky flavor
- Once the chip bay is ready, load up your marinated meat onto the grill directly
- The stainless steel rack is made for direct smoking, however, if you wish they you can use a stainless steel container to avoid drippings
- Once the meat is in place, lock the door of the chamber
- Turn your smoker "On" using the specified button and adjust the temperature
- Wait until it is done!

Keep in mind that the above-mentioned steps are merely the basic ones; different recipes might call for different steps to follow.

Either way, they won't be much complicated as well!

THINGS TO KEEP IN MIND WHEN BUYING YOUR FIRST ELECTRIC SMOKER!

Buying an Electric Smoker is by no means an easy investment. They are generally quite expensive and require a lot of effort and dedication to get one. Due to the sheer variety of Electric Smokers though, it sometimes gets really difficult for an individual to find and purchase the one that is best for their needs. Especially if that individual is a complete beginner in this field. I wanted to make sure that you don't fall victim to such an event, as the feeling of making an unsatisfactory purchase is all but joyful! Therefore, in the following section, I have broken down the key elements that you should keep an eye out for while making your first Electric Smoker purchase. After this section, you will also find a list of the Top 10 Electric Smoker (At the time writing) that your money can buy!

That being said, here are the factors to consider.

Price: This is perhaps the most decisive part of your purchase. Always make sure to do a lot of research in order to find the best one that falls within your budget (the provided list will help you). However, you should keep in mind that going for the cheapest one might not be a good idea!

As much tempting as they might sound, the quality of the build materials and the finished meal won't be up to mark.

Asides from that, things to keep in mind include

- The reviews
- Safety ratings
- Warranty of the device

Capacity: Electric smokers come in different sizes and you are bound to find one that will suit your need. Before purchasing your Electric Smoker, the things that you should consider in terms of capacity include:

- Decide the place where you are going to keep your smoker and hot it will be stored
- Assess the size of your family and how much meat you are going to cook in each batch

Depending on your smoking experience, you are going to need a larger capacity smoker if you tend to throw a lot of events! But if it's for personal use, then a reasonably small sized one will do.

Brand: At the time of writing, Bradley and Masterbuilt were on the forefront of the Electric Smoker market. However, there are some other brands such as Smoke Hollow, Esinkin, and Char-Broil.

A good idea is to not rely on a brand too much, but rather look at the specific models and assess the one that suits your needs (depending on the features of the smoker)

Durability: Always make sure that you don't sacrifice on the durability of the device (even if it costs an extra dollar)!

As mentioned earlier, a Smoker is an expensive investment and you want to buy one that will last you for years to come.

Two of the biggest issues when it comes to durability that you should keep in mind are

- The quality of the thermostat
- Quality of the seal

If your smoker is properly sealed up, then it will require less heat to control and prevent the smoke from escaping. This will allow the veggies and meat to be penetrated by the smoke evenly, giving more delicious meals.

Safe and Accessibility: Regardless of the fact that you are an experienced smoker or a beginner, always make sure to read through every single functionality of the smoker that you are considering. Read the provided manufacturers guide to better educate yourself on the smoker and assess how safe and accessible the smoker might be for you. (According to your experience level)

CONCLUSION

I can't express how honored I am to think that you found my book interesting and informative enough to read it all through to the end. I thank you again for purchasing this book and I hope that you had as much fun reading it as I had writing it. I bid you farewell and encourage you to move forward and find your true Smoked Meat spirit!

OTHER BOOKS BY ADAM JONES

https://www.amazon.com/dp/1548040959

https://www.amazon.com/dp/1979559902

https://www.amazon.com/dp/1544791178

https://www.amazon.com/dp/1979811318

https://www.amazon.com/dp/1546605916

https://www.amazon.com/dp/1977677347

https://www.amazon.com/dp/1542597846

https://www.amazon.com/dp/154418199X

My Amazon page:
www.amazon.com/author/adjones

Made in the USA
San Bernardino, CA
13 February 2018